MW00876472

THE PRAYER
MAP

A
CREATIVE
JOURNAL

BARBOUR BOOKS
An Imprint of Barbour Publishing, Inc.

Published by Barbour Books, an imprint of Barbour Publishing, Inc., 1810 Barbour Drive, Uhrichsville, Ohio 44683, www.barbourbooks.com

Our mission is to inspire the world with the life-changing message of the Bible.

Member of the
Evangelical Christian
Publishers Association

Printed in China.
000700   0521   DS

What does prayer look like?

What kinds of things should I pray about?

Do my prayers matter to God?

And does He really hear every word I pray?

Discover the power of prayer with this fun and creative prayer journal that guides you to create your very own prayer map—as you write out specific thoughts, ideas, and lists, which you can follow (from start to finish!)—as you talk to God. (Be sure to write the date on each one of your prayer maps so you can look back over time and see how God is working in your life!)

The Prayer Map journal will not only encourage you to spend time talking with God about the things that matter most (to you and to Him!). . .it will also help you make daily prayer a habit—for life!

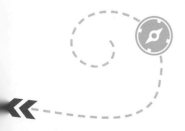

Date:

START HERE

Dear God, ...
....
....
....
....

I'M THANKFUL FOR. . . ..
....
....
....
....
....
....
....

MY WORRIES. . .
....
....
....
....
....
....
....
....
....
....
....
....
....
....

People I am praying for. . .
....
....
....
....
....
....

....
....
....
....
....

MY NEEDS. . .

....
....
....
....
....
....
....
....
....
....
....
....

►► Other stuff I need
to share with You, God. . .

66

....
....
....
....
....

99

AMEN.
*Thank You, God,
for hearing my prayers!*

*"O Lord, hear the prayer of Your servant
and the prayer of Your servants who
are happy to fear Your name."*

NEHEMIAH 1:11

Date: .... START HERE

Dear God, ...
....
....
....
....

I'M THANKFUL FOR. . . ..
....
....
....
....
....
....
....

People I am praying for. . .
....
....
....
....
....
....

MY WORRIES. . .

....
....
....
....
....
....
....
....
....
....
....
....
....

>> HERE'S WHAT'S GOING ON IN MY LIFE. . .

....
....
....
....
....
....

MY NEEDS. . .

....
....
....
....
....
....
....
....
....
....
....
....

Other stuff I need
to share with You, God. . .

"

....

....

....

....

....

"

AMEN.
*Thank You, God,
for hearing my prayers!*

*The prayer from the heart. . .
right with God has much power.*

JAMES 5:16

Date:

Dear God, ...
....
....
....
....

I'M THANKFUL FOR. . . ..
....
....
....
....
....
....

MY WORRIES. . .
....
....
....
....
....
....
....
....
....
....
....
....

People I am praying for. . .
....
....
....
....
....
....

....
....
....
....
....

MY NEEDS. . .

....
....
....
....
....
....
....
....
....
....
....
....

❯❯ Other stuff I need
to share with You, God. . .

"

....
....
....
....
....
....

"

AMEN.
*Thank You, God,
for hearing my prayers!*

*Listen to my cry for help, my King
and my God. For I pray to you.*

PSALM 5:2

Date:

START HERE

Dear God, ...
....
....
....
....

I'M THANKFUL FOR. . . ..
....
....
....
....
....
....

MY WORRIES. . .
....
....
....
....
....
....
....
....
....
....
....

People I am praying for. . .
....
....
....
....
....

HERE'S WHAT'S GOING ON IN MY LIFE. . .

....

....

....

....

....

MY NEEDS. . .

....

....

....

....

....

....

....

....

....

....

....

....

Other stuff I need
to share with You, God. . .

"

....

....

....

....

....

....

"

AMEN.
*Thank You, God,
for hearing my prayers!*

*Pray that the Word of the Lord will go
out over all the land and prove its power.*

2 THESSALONIANS 3:1

Date: START HERE

Dear God,

I'M THANKFUL FOR. . .

MY WORRIES. . .

People I am praying for. . .

▶▶ HERE'S WHAT'S GOING ON IN MY LIFE. . .

....

....

....

....

....

MY NEEDS. . .

....

....

....

....

....

....

....

....

....

....

....

....

Other stuff I need
to share with You, God. . .

66

....

....

....

....

....

....

99

AMEN.
*Thank You, God,
for hearing my prayers!*

*"Ask, and what you are asking for will be given
to you. Look, and what you are looking for you
will find. Knock, and the door you are
knocking on will be opened to you."*

MATTHEW 7:7

Date:

START HERE

Dear God, ...
....
....
....
....

I'M THANKFUL FOR. . ...
....
....
....
....
....
....
....

People I am praying for. . .
....
....
....
....
....

MY WORRIES...
....
....
....
....
....
....
....
....
....
....
....
....

....
....
....
....
....

MY NEEDS...

....
....
....
....
....
....
....
....
....
....
....
....

Other stuff I need
to share with You, God...

66

....
....
....
....
....
....

99

AMEN.
*Thank You, God,
for hearing my prayers!*

*O Lord, listen to my cry.
Show loving-kindness to me and answer me.*

PSALM 27:7

Date: _____ START HERE

Dear God, ...
....
....
....
....

I'M THANKFUL FOR. . . ..
....

MY WORRIES. . .
....
....
....
....
....
....
....
....

People I am praying for. . .
....
....
....
....
....
....

HERE'S WHAT'S GOING ON IN MY LIFE. . .

....

....

....

....

....

MY NEEDS. . .

....

....

....

....

....

....

....

....

....

....

....

....

Other stuff I need
to share with You, God. . .

"

....

....

....

....

....

"

AMEN.
*Thank You, God,
for hearing my prayers!*

*You must keep praying. Keep watching!
Be thankful always.*

COLOSSIANS 4:2

Date: _____ → START HERE

Dear God, ...
....
....
....
....

I'M THANKFUL FOR. . . ..
....
....
....
....
....
....
....

MY WORRIES. . .
....
....
....
....
....
....
....
....
....
....
....
....

People I am praying for. . .
....
....
....
....
....

HERE'S WHAT'S GOING ON IN MY LIFE...

....

....

....

....

....

MY NEEDS...

....

....

....

....

....

....

....

....

....

....

....

....

Other stuff I need
to share with You, God...

"
....

....

....

....

....

"

AMEN.
*Thank You, God,
for hearing my prayers!*

*"O Lord, You are great and we fear You. You keep
Your agreement and show loving-kindness to
those who love You and keep Your Laws."*

DANIEL 9:4

Date: START HERE

Dear God, ...
....
....
....
....

I'M THANKFUL FOR. . . ..
....
....
....
....
....
....
....

People I am praying for. . .
....
....
....
....
....

MY WORRIES. . .
....
....
....
....
....
....
....
....
....
....
....
....
....
....

HERE'S WHAT'S GOING ON IN MY LIFE. . .

....

....

....

....

....

MY NEEDS. . .

....

....

....

....

....

....

....

....

....

....

....

....

Other stuff I need
to share with You, God. . .

"

....

....

....

....

....

"

AMEN.
*Thank You, God,
for hearing my prayers!*

*The Lord will send His loving-kindness in the
day. And His song will be with me in the night,
a prayer to the God of my life.*

PSALM 42:8

Date:

START HERE

Dear God, ...
....
....
....
....

I'M THANKFUL FOR. . . ..
....
....
....
....
....
....
....

MY WORRIES. . .
....
....
....
....
....
....
....
....
....
....
....
....

People I am praying for. . .
....
....
....
....
....
....

≫ HERE'S WHAT'S GOING ON IN MY LIFE. . .

....

....

....

....

....

MY NEEDS. . .

....

....

....

....

....

....

....

....

....

....

....

....

....

....

≫ Other stuff I need
to share with You, God. . .

"

....

....

....

....

....

....

....

"

AMEN.
Thank You, God,
for hearing my prayers!

Our hope comes from God. May He fill you with joy
and peace because of your trust in Him. May your
hope grow stronger by the power of the Holy Spirit.

ROMANS 15:13

Date:

START HERE

Dear God, ...
....
....
....
....

I'M THANKFUL FOR. . . ..
....
....
....
....
....
....

MY WORRieS. . .
....
....
....
....
....
....
....
....
....
....
....

People I am praying for. . .
....
....
....
....
....

HERE'S WHAT'S GOING ON IN MY LIFE. . .

....
....
....
....
....

MY NEEDS. . .

....
....
....
....
....
....
....
....
....
....
....
....

Other stuff I need
to share with You, God. . .

"

....
....
....
....
....

"

AMEN.
*Thank You, God,
for hearing my prayers!*

*"Do not stop crying to
the Lord our God for us."*

1 SAMUEL 7:8

Date:

START HERE

Dear God, ...
....
....
....
....

I'M THANKFUL FOR. . . ..
....
....
....
....
....
....

MY WORRIES. . .
....
....
....
....
....
....
....
....
....
....
....
....
....

People I am praying for. . .
....
....
....
....
....

HERE'S WHAT'S GOING ON IN MY LIFE...

....
....
....
....
....

MY NEEDS...

....
....
....
....
....
....
....
....
....
....
....
....

Other stuff I need to share with You, God...

66

....
....
....
....
....
....
....

99

AMEN.
*Thank You, God,
for hearing my prayers!*

*We always pray and give thanks to God for you.
He is the Father of our Lord Jesus Christ.*

COLOSSIANS 1:3

Date: **START HERE**

Dear God, ...
....
....
....
....

I'M THANKFUL FOR. . . ..
....
....
....
....
....
....
....

MY WORRieS. . .

....
....
....
....
....
....
....
....
....
....
....
....
....
....

People I am praying for. . .
....
....
....
....
....
....

HERE'S WHAT'S GOING ON IN MY LIFE. . .

....

....

....

....

....

MY NEEDS. . .

....

....

....

....

....

....

....

....

....

....

....

....

....

Other stuff I need
to share with You, God. . .

66

....

....

....

....

....

....

99

AMEN.
*Thank You, God,
for hearing my prayers!*

*First of all, I ask you to pray much for all
[people] and to give thanks for them.*

1 TIMOTHY 2:1

Date:

START HERE

Dear God, ...
....
....
....
....

I'M THANKFUL FOR. . . ..
....
....
....
....
....
....
....

MY WORRIES. . .
....
....
....
....
....
....
....
....
....
....
....
....
....
....

People I am praying for. . .
....
....
....
....
....

HERE'S WHAT'S GOING ON IN MY LIFE...

....

....

....

....

....

MY NEEDS...

....

....

....

....

....

....

....

....

....

....

....

....

....

Other stuff I need
to share with You, God...

"

....

....

....

....

....

"

AMEN.
*Thank You, God,
for hearing my prayers!*

*Answer me, O Lord,
for Your loving-kindness is good.*

PSALM 69:16

Date: .... **START HERE**

Dear God, ...
....
....
....
....

I'M THANKFUL FOR. . . ..
....
....
....
....
....
....
....

MY WORRIES. . .
....
....
....
....
....
....
....
....
....
....
....
....
....

People I am praying for. . .
....
....
....
....
....

HERE'S WHAT'S GOING ON IN MY LIFE. . .

....

....

....

....

....

MY NEEDS. . .

....

....

....

....

....

....

....

....

....

....

....

....

Other stuff I need
to share with You, God. . .

"

....

....

....

....

....

"

AMEN.
*Thank You, God,
for hearing my prayers!*

*They will pray for you with great love because
God has given you His loving-favor.*

2 CORINTHIANS 9:14

Date: START HERE

Dear God,

I'M THANKFUL FOR. . .

MY WORRIES. . .

People I am praying for. . .

....
....
....
....
....

MY NEEDS...

....
....
....
....
....
....
....
....
....
....
....
....

Other stuff I need
to share with You, God...

66

....
....
....
....
....
....

99

AMEN.
*Thank You, God,
for hearing my prayers!*

*I will call on Him as long as I live,
because He has turned His ear to me.*
PSALM 116:2

Date: START HERE

Dear God, ...
....
....
....
....

I'M THANKFUL FOR. . . ..
....
....
....
....
....
....
....

People I am praying for. . .
....
....
....
....
....
....

MY WORRieS. . .
....
....
....
....
....
....
....
....
....
....
....
....
....
....
....
....

....

....

....

....

....

MY NEEDS...

....
....
....
....
....
....
....
....
....
....
....

Other stuff I need
to share with You, God...

"

....

....

....

....

"

AMEN.
*Thank You, God,
for hearing my prayers!*

*I pray that because of the riches of His
shining-greatness, He will make you strong with
power in your hearts through the Holy Spirit.*

EPHESIANS 3:16

Date: _____ **START HERE**

Dear God, ...
....
....
....
....

I'M THANKFUL FOR. . ...
....
....
....
....
....
....
....

MY WORRIES...
....
....
....
....
....
....
....
....
....
....
....
....

People I am praying for. . .
....
....
....
....
....
....

HERE'S WHAT'S GOING ON IN MY LIFE. . .

....
....
....
....
....

MY NEEDS. . .

....
....
....
....
....
....
....
....
....
....
....
....
....

Other stuff I need
to share with You, God. . .

66

....
....
....
....
....
....

99

AMEN.
*Thank You, God,
for hearing my prayers!*

*"O Lord, God of Israel, there is no God like You
in heaven or on earth. You keep Your promises
and show loving-kindness to Your servants who
walk with You with all their hearts."*

2 CHRONICLES 6:14

Date: .... START HERE

Dear God, ...
....
....
....
....

I'M THANKFUL FOR. . . ..
....
....
....
....
....
....
....

MY WORRIES. . .
....
....
....
....
....
....
....
....
....
....
....
....
....
....

People I am praying for. . .
....
....
....
....
....
....

HERE'S WHAT'S GOING ON IN MY LIFE. . .

....

....

....

....

....

MY NEEDS. . .

....

....

....

....

....

....

....

....

....

....

....

....

....

Other stuff I need
to share with You, God. . .

"

....

....

....

....

....

....

....

....

"

AMEN.
*Thank You, God,
for hearing my prayers!*

*The Good News tells us we are made right
with God by faith in Him. Then, by faith
we live that new life through Him.*

ROMANS 1:17

Date: .... **START HERE**

Dear God, ...
....
....
....
....

I'M THANKFUL FOR. . . ..
....
....
....
....
....
....
....

MY WORRieS. . .
....
....
....
....
....
....
....
....
....
....
....
....
....
....

People I am praying for. . .
....
....
....
....
....

....
....
....
....
....

MY NEEDS...

....
....
....
....
....
....
....
....
....
....
....

Other stuff I need
to share with You, God...

66

....
....
....
....
....

99

AMEN.
*Thank You, God,
for hearing my prayers!*

*I put out my hands to You.
My soul is thirsty for You like a dry land.*

PSALM 143:6

Date: START HERE

Dear God, ...
....
....
....
....

I'M THANKFUL FOR. . . ..
....
....
....
....
....
....
....

People I am praying for. . .
....
....
....
....
....
....

MY WORRIES. . .
....
....
....
....
....
....
....
....
....
....
....
....
....

HERE'S WHAT'S GOING ON IN MY LIFE. . .

....

....

....

....

....

MY NEEDS. . .

....

....

....

....

....

....

....

....

....

....

....

....

Other stuff I need
to share with You, God. . .

"

....

....

....

....

....

....

"

AMEN.
*Thank You, God,
for hearing my prayers!*

*"Respect and give thanks for those who
try to bring bad to you. Pray for those
who make it very hard for you."*

LUKE 6:28

Date:

START HERE

Dear God, ...
....
....
....
....

I'M THANKFUL FOR. . . ..
....
....
....
....
....
....
....

MY WORRIES. . .
....
....
....
....
....
....
....
....
....
....
....
....
....
....

People I am praying for. . .
....
....
....
....
....
....

HeRe'S WHAT'S GOING ON IN MY LIFe. . .

....
....
....
....
....

MY NEEDS. . .

....
....
....
....
....
....
....
....
....
....
....
....
....

Other stuff I need
to share with You, God. . .

"

....
....
....
....
....
....
....

"

AMEN.
*Thank You, God,
for hearing my prayers!*

*I pray that your love will grow more and
more. I pray that you will have better
understanding and be wise in all things.*

PHILIPPIANS 1:9

Date: START HERE

Dear God, ...
....
....
....
....

I'M THANKFUL FOR.. . ...
....
....
....
....
....
....
....

MY WORRIES...
....
....
....
....
....
....
....
....
....
....
....
....
....
....

People I am praying for. . .
....
....
....
....
....
....

HERE'S WHAT'S GOING ON IN MY LIFE. . .

....
....
....
....
....

MY NEEDS. . .

....
....
....
....
....
....
....
....
....
....
....
....

Other stuff I need
to share with You, God. . .

66

....
....
....
....
....
....

99

AMEN.
*Thank You, God,
for hearing my prayers!*

*"But I tell you, love those who hate you. . . .
Pray for those who do bad things to you."*

MATTHEW 5:44

Date: START HERE

Dear God, ...
....
....
....
....

I'M THANKFUL FOR. . . ..
....
....
....
....
....
....

MY WORRIES. . .
....
....
....
....
....
....
....
....
....
....
....
....
....

People I am praying for. . .
....
....
....
....
....

⟫⟫ HERE'S WHAT'S GOING ON IN MY LIFE...

....
....
....
....
.... ⟫⟫

MY NEEDS...

....
....
....
....
....
....
....
....
....
....
....
....
....

⟫⟫ Other stuff I need
to share with You, God...

"

....
....
....
....
....
....

"

AMEN.
*Thank You, God,
for hearing my prayers!*

*O Lord, I will give thanks to You among the
people. I will sing praises to You among the
nations. For Your loving-kindness is great
to the heavens, and Your truth to the clouds.*

PSALM 57:9–10

Date: .... START HERE

Dear God, ...
....
....
....
....

I'M THANKFUL FOR. . . ..
....
....
....
....
....
....

MY WORRIES. . .
....
....
....
....
....
....
....
....
....
....
....
....
....
....

People I am praying for. . .
....
....
....
....
....
....

HERE'S WHAT'S GOING ON IN MY LIFE. . .

....
....
....
....
....

MY NEEDS. . .

....
....
....
....
....
....
....
....
....
....
....
....
....

Other stuff I need
to share with You, God. . .

66

....
....
....
....
....

99

AMEN.
*Thank You, God,
for hearing my prayers!*

*O Lord, to You I call.
O my Rock, listen to me.*
PSALM 28:1

Date: .... START HERE

Dear God, ...
....
....
....
....

I'M THANKFUL FOR. . . ..
....
....
....
....
....
....

MY WORRIES. . .
....
....
....
....
....
....
....
....
....
....
....
....
....
....

People I am praying for. . .
....
....
....
....
....
....

HERE'S WHAT'S GOING ON IN MY LIFE. . .

....

....

....

....

....

MY NEEDS. . .

....

....

....

....

....

....

....

....

....

....

....

....

....

" Other stuff I need
to share with You, God. . .

....

....

....

....

....

....

"

AMEN.
*Thank You, God,
for hearing my prayers!*

*I pray that you will know how great His power
is for those who have put their trust in Him.*

Ephesians 1:19

Date:

START HERE

Dear God,

I'M THANKFUL FOR. . .

MY WORRIES. . .

People I am praying for. . .

....
....
....
....
....

MY NEEDS. . .

....
....
....
....
....
....
....
....
....
....
....

▶▶ Other stuff I need
to share with You, God. . .

66

....
....
....
....
....
....

99

AMEN.
*Thank You, God,
for hearing my prayers!*

*"All things you ask for in prayer,
you will receive if you have faith."*

MATTHEW 21:22

Date: **START HERE**

Dear God, ...
....
....
....

I'M THANKFUL FOR. . . ..
....
....
....
....
....
....

People I am praying for. . .
....
....
....
....
....
....

MY WORRIES . . .
....
....
....
....
....
....
....
....
....
....
....
....
....

HERE'S WHAT'S GOING ON IN MY LIFE. . .

....

....

....

....

....

MY NEEDS. . .

....
....
....
....
....
....
....
....
....
....
....
....
....

Other stuff I need
to share with You, God. . .

"

....

....

....

....

....

"

AMEN.
*Thank You, God,
for hearing my prayers!*

*Answer me with Your saving truth in
Your great loving-kindness, O God.*

PSALM 69:13

Date: **START HERE**

Dear God, ...
....
....
....
....

I'M THANKFUL FOR. . ...
....
....
....
....
....
....
....

MY WORRIES. . .
....
....
....
....
....
....
....
....
....
....

People I am praying for. . .
....
....
....
....
....
....

HERE'S WHAT'S GOING ON IN MY LIFE. . .

....

....

....

....

....

MY NEEDS. . .

....

....

....

....

....

....

....

....

....

....

....

....

Other stuff I need
to share with You, God. . .

"

....

....

....

....

....

....

"

AMEN.
*Thank You, God,
for hearing my prayers!*

*But as for me, it is good to be near God.
I have made the Lord God my safe place.
So I may tell of all the things You have done.*

PSALM 73:28

Date: _____ START HERE

Dear God, ...
....
....
....
....

I'M THANKFUL FOR. . . ..
....
....
....
....
....
....
....

MY WORRIES. . .
....
....
....
....
....
....
....
....
....
....
....
....
....

People I am praying for. . .
....
....
....
....
....
....

HERE'S WHAT'S GOING ON IN MY LIFE. . .

....
....
....
....
....

MY NEEDS. . .

....
....
....
....
....
....
....
....
....
....
....
....
....

**Other stuff I need
to share with You, God. . .**

66

....
....
....
....
....
....
....

99

AMEN.
*Thank You, God,
for hearing my prayers!*

*Then [Jesus] went away by
Himself to pray in a desert.*
LUKE 5:16

Date: **START HERE**

Dear God, ...
....
....
....
....

I'M THANKFUL FOR. . . ..
....
....
....
....
....
....

MY WORRIES. . .
....
....
....
....
....
....
....
....
....
....
....
....

People I am praying for. . .
....
....
....
....
....
....

▶▶ HERE'S WHAT'S GOING ON IN MY LIFE. . .

....

....

....

....

....

MY NEEDS. . .

....

....

....

....

....

....

....

....

....

....

....

....

Other stuff I need
to share with You, God. . .

"

....

....

....

....

....

....

"

AMEN.
*Thank You, God,
for hearing my prayers!*

*I will sing of the loving-kindness of the Lord
forever. I will make known with my mouth
how faithful You are to all people.*

PSALM 89:1

Date:

START HERE

Dear God, ...
....
....
....
....

I'M THANKFUL FOR. . . ..
....
....
....
....
....
....

MY WORRIES. . .
....
....
....
....
....
....
....
....
....
....
....
....

People I am praying for. . .
....
....
....
....
....

HERE'S WHAT'S GOING ON IN MY LIFE. . .

....

....

....

....

....

MY NEEDS. . .

....

....

....

....

....

....

....

....

....

....

....

....

Other stuff I need
to share with You, God. . .

66

....

....

....

....

....

99

AMEN.
*Thank You, God,
for hearing my prayers!*

*Honor and thanks be to God! He has not
turned away from my prayer or held
His loving-kindness from me.*

PSALM 66:20

Date:

START HERE

Dear God, ...
....
....
....
....

I'M THANKFUL FOR. . . ..
....
....
....
....
....
....
....

MY WORRieS. . .
....
....
....
....
....
....
....
....
....
....
....
....
....

People I am praying for. . .
....
....
....
....
....
....

➤➤ HERE'S WHAT'S GOING ON IN MY LIFE. . .

....
....
....
....
....

MY NEEDS. . .

....
....
....
....
....
....
....
....
....
....
....
....

➤➤ *Other stuff I need
to share with You, God. . .*

❝

....
....
....
....
....
....

❞

AMEN.
*Thank You, God,
for hearing my prayers!*

*The Holy Spirit helps us where we are weak.
We do not know how to pray or what we should
pray for, but the Holy Spirit prays to God for
us with sounds that cannot be put into words.*

ROMANS 8:26

Date: _____ **START HERE**

Dear God, ...
....
....
....
....

I'M THANKFUL FOR. . . ..
....
....
....
....
....
....
....

People I am praying for. . .
....
....
....
....
....

MY WORRIES. . .
....
....
....
....
....
....
....
....
....
....
....

HERE'S WHAT'S GOING ON IN MY LIFE...

....

....

....

....

....

MY NEEDS...

....

....

....

....

....

....

....

....

....

....

....

....

Other stuff I need
to share with You, God...

"

....

....

....

....

....

....

"

AMEN.
*Thank You, God,
for hearing my prayers!*

*Be happy in your hope. Do not give
up when trouble comes. Do not let
anything stop you from praying.*

ROMANS 12:12

Date:

START HERE

Dear God,

I'M THANKFUL FOR. . .

MY WORRIES. . .

People I am praying for. . .

HERE'S WHAT'S GOING ON IN MY LIFE. . .

MY NEEDS. . .

Other stuff I need
to share with You, God. . .

"

"

AMEN.
*Thank You, God,
for hearing my prayers!*

*So my soul may sing praise to You,
and not be quiet. O Lord my God,
I will give thanks to You forever.*

PSALM 30:12

Date: _____ START HERE

Dear God, ...
....
....
....
....

I'M THANKFUL FOR. . . ..
....
....
....
....
....
....
....

MY WORRIES. . .
....
....
....
....
....
....
....
....
....
....
....
....
....

People I am praying for. . .
....
....
....
....
....

HERE'S WHAT'S GOING ON IN MY LIFE...

MY NEEDS...

Other stuff I need
to share with You, God...

66

99

AMEN.
*Thank You, God,
for hearing my prayers!*

*I have called to You, O God, for You will
answer me. Listen to me and hear my words.*

PSALM 17:6

Date: START HERE

📍 Dear God, ...
....
....
....
....

I'M THANKFUL FOR. . . ..
....
....
....
....
....
....

MY WORRieS. . .
....
....
....
....
....
....
....
....
....
....
....
....

People I am praying for. . .
....
....
....
....
....

▶▶ HERE'S WHAT'S GOING ON IN MY LIFE. . .

....

....

....

....

....

MY NEEDS. . .

....

....

....

....

....

....

....

....

....

....

....

....

Other stuff I need
to share with You, God. . .

"

....

....

....

....

....

"

AMEN.
*Thank You, God,
for hearing my prayers!*

You also help us by praying for us.
Many people thank God for His favor to us.
This is an answer to the prayers of many people.

2 CORINTHIANS 1:11

Date: .... **START HERE**

Dear God, ...
....
....
....
....

I'M THANKFUL FOR. . . ..
....
....
....
....
....
....

MY WORRIES. . .
....
....
....
....
....
....
....

People I am praying for. . .
....
....
....
....
....
....
....
....
....
....
....

Here's what's going on in my life...

....

....

....

....

....

MY NEEDS...

....

....

....

....

....

....

....

....

....

....

....

....

Other stuff I need
to share with You, God...

"

....

....

....

....

....

....

"

AMEN.
*Thank You, God,
for hearing my prayers!*

*I love the Lord, because He
hears my voice and my prayers.*

PSALM 116:1

Date:

START HERE

Dear God, ...
....
....
....
....

I'M THANKFUL FOR. . . ..
....
....
....
....
....
....

MY WORRIES. . .
....
....
....
....
....
....
....
....
....
....
....
....
....

People I am praying for. . .
....
....
....
....
....

HERE'S WHAT'S GOING ON IN MY LIFE. . .

....

....

....

....

....

MY NEEDS. . .

....

....

....

....

....

....

....

....

....

....

....

....

....

66

Other stuff I need
to share with You, God. . .

....

....

....

....

....

99

AMEN.
*Thank You, God,
for hearing my prayers!*

I always give thanks for you and pray for you.

EPHESIANS 1:16

Date:

START HERE

Dear God, ...
....
....
....
....

I'M THANKFUL FOR. . . ..
....
....
....
....
....
....
....

MY WORRIES. . .
....
....
....
....
....
....
....
....
....
....
....
....
....

People I am praying for. . .
....
....
....
....
....

HERE'S WHAT'S GOING ON IN MY LIFE. . .

....

....

....

....

....

MY NEEDS. . .

....

....

....

....

....

....

....

....

....

....

....

....

....

" Other stuff I need
to share with You, God. . .

....

....

....

....

....

....

AMEN.
*Thank You, God,
for hearing my prayers!*
"

*The Lord is my strength and my safe cover.
My heart trusts in Him, and I am helped. So my
heart is full of joy. I will thank Him with my song.*

PSALM 28:7

Date: _____ START HERE

Dear God, ...
....
....
....
....

I'M THANKFUL FOR. . . ..
....
....
....
....
....
....

People I am praying for. . .
....
....
....
....
....
....

MY WORRIES. . .
....
....
....
....
....
....
....
....
....
....
....
....
....

›› HERE'S WHAT'S GOING ON IN MY LIFE. . .

....

....

....

....

.... ››

MY NEEDS. . .

....

....

....

....

....

....

....

....

....

....

....

....

Other stuff I need
to share with You, God. . .

"

....

....

....

....

....

....

"

AMEN.
*Thank You, God,
for hearing my prayers!*

*I will give You thanks forever because of what You
have done. And I will hope in Your name, for it is
good to be where those who belong to You are.*

PSALM 52:9

Date: **START HERE**

Dear God, ...
....
....
....
....

I'M THANKFUL FOR. . . ..
....
....
....
....
....
....
....

MY WORRIES...
....
....
....
....
....
....
....
....
....
....
....
....
....

People I am praying for. . .
....
....
....
....
....
....

HERE'S WHAT'S GOING ON IN MY LIFE...

....

....

....

....

....

MY NEEDS...

....

....

....

....

....

....

....

....

....

....

....

....

Other stuff I need
to share with You, God...

"

....

....

....

....

....

....

"

AMEN.
*Thank You, God,
for hearing my prayers!*

*O God Who saves us, You answer us in the way that
is right and good by Your great works that make
people stand in fear. You are the hope of all the
ends of the earth and of the farthest seas.*

PSALM 65:5

Date:

START HERE

Dear God, ...
....
....
....
....

I'M THANKFUL FOR. . . ..
....
....
....
....
....
....
....

People I am praying for. . .
....
....
....
....
....
....

MY WORRieS. . .
....
....
....
....
....
....
....
....
....
....
....
....
....
....

▶▶ HERE'S WHAT'S GOING ON IN MY LIFE. . .

MY NEEDS. . .

Other stuff I need
to share with You, God. . .

"

"

AMEN.
*Thank You, God,
for hearing my prayers!*

*You must pray at all times as the Holy Spirit
leads you to pray. Pray for the things that are
needed. You must watch and keep on praying.
Remember to pray for all Christians.*

EPHESIANS 6:18

Date: **START HERE**

Dear God, ...
....
....
....
....

I'M THANKFUL FOR. . . ..
....
....
....
....
....
....

MY WORRIES. . .
....
....
....
....
....
....
....
....
....
....
....
....
....
....

People I am praying for. . .
....
....
....
....
....
....

>> HERE'S WHAT'S GOING ON IN MY LIFE...

....

....

....

....

.... >>

MY NEEDS...

....

....

....

....

....

....

....

....

....

....

....

....

....

>> Other stuff I need
to share with You, God...

66

....

....

....

....

....

....

99

AMEN.
*Thank You, God,
for hearing my prayers!*

*O Lord of all, how happy is
the [person] who trusts in You!*

PSALM 84:12

Dear God, ...
....
....
....
....

I'M THANKFUL FOR. . . ..
....
....
....
....
....
....
....

MY WORRIES. . .
....
....
....
....
....
....
....
....
....
....
....

People I am praying for. . .
....
....
....
....
....

HERE'S WHAT'S GOING ON IN MY LIFE...

....

....

....

....

....

MY NEEDS...

....

....

....

....

....

....

....

....

....

....

....

....

Other stuff I need
to share with You, God...

"

....

....

....

....

....

"

AMEN.
*Thank You, God,
for hearing my prayers!*

I always have joy as I pray for all of you.
PHILIPPIANS 1:4

Date: .... **START HERE**

Dear God, ...
....
....
....
....

I'M THANKFUL FOR. . . ..
....
....
....
....
....
....
....

MY WORRIES. . .
....
....
....
....
....
....
....
....
....
....
....
....
....

People I am praying for. . .
....
....
....
....
....

HERE'S WHAT'S GOING ON IN MY LIFE. . .

....
....
....
....
....

MY NEEDS. . .

....
....
....
....
....
....
....
....
....
....
....
....

Other stuff I need
to share with You, God. . .

"
....
....
....
....
....

"

AMEN.
*Thank You, God,
for hearing my prayers!*

*"When you stand to pray, if you have anything
against anyone, forgive him. Then your Father
in heaven will forgive your sins also."*

MARK 11:25

Date: **START HERE**

Dear God, ...
....
....
....
....

I'M THANKFUL FOR. . . ..
....
....
....
....
....
....

MY WORRIES. . .
....
....
....
....
....
....
....
....
....
....
....

People I am praying for. . .
....
....
....
....
....
....

▶▶ HERE'S WHAT'S GOING ON IN MY LIFE. . .

....

....

....

....

....

MY NEEDS. . .

....

....

....

....

....

....

....

....

....

....

....

....

Other stuff I need
to share with You, God. . .

66

....

....

....

....

....

....

99

AMEN.
*Thank You, God,
for hearing my prayers!*

*Do not worry. Learn to pray about
everything. Give thanks to God as
you ask Him for what you need.*

PHILIPPIANS 4:6

START HERE

Dear God, ...
....
....
....
....

I'M THANKFUL FOR. . . ..
....
....
....
....
....
....
....

MY WORRIES. . .
....
....
....
....
....
....
....
....
....
....
....
....
....
....

People I am praying for. . .
....
....
....
....

....

....
....
....
....
....

MY NEEDS. . .

....
....
....
....
....
....
....
....
....
....
....
....

Other stuff I need
to share with You, God. . .

"

....
....
....
....
....
....

"

AMEN.
*Thank You, God,
for hearing my prayers!*

*I pray that our faith together will
help you know all the good things
you have through Christ Jesus.*

PHILEMON 1:6

Date:

START HERE

Dear God, ...
....
....
....
....

I'M THANKFUL FOR. . . ..
....
....
....
....
....
....
....

MY WORRIES. . .
....
....
....
....
....
....
....
....
....
....
....
....
....

People I am praying for. . .
....
....
....
....
....
....

≫ HERE'S WHAT'S GOING ON IN MY LIFE. . .

....
....
....
....
.... ≫

MY NEEDS. . .

....
....
....
....
....
....
....
....
....
....
....
....

≫ Other stuff I need
to share with You, God. . .

"
....
....
....
....
....
....

"
AMEN.
*Thank You, God,
for hearing my prayers!*

*I have never stopped praying for you since I heard
about you. I ask God that you may know what He
wants you to do. I ask God to fill you with the wisdom
and understanding the Holy Spirit gives.*

COLOSSIANS 1:9

Date: .... **START HERE**

Dear God, ...
....
....
....
....

I'M THANKFUL FOR. . . ..
....
....
....
....
....
....
....

MY WORRIES. . .
....
....
....
....
....
....
....
....
....
....
....
....
....
....
....
....
....

People I am praying for. . .
....
....
....
....
....
....

....
....
....
....
....

MY NEEDS. . .

....
....
....
....
....
....
....
....
....
....
....
....
....

Other stuff I need
to share with You, God. . .

"

....
....
....
....
....
....

"

AMEN.
*Thank You, God,
for hearing my prayers!*

*So I will give honor to You as long as I live.
I will lift up my hands in Your name.*

PSALM 63:4

Date:

START HERE

Dear God, ...
....
....
....
....

I'M THANKFUL FOR. . . ..
....
....
....
....
....
....

MY WORRIES. . .
....
....
....
....
....
....
....
....
....
....
....
....
....
....

People I am praying for. . .
....
....
....
....
....
....

MY NEEDS. . .

Other stuff I need
to share with You, God. . .

"

"

AMEN.
*Thank You, God,
for hearing my prayers!*

*"Pray like this: 'Our Father in heaven,
Your name is holy.'"*

MATTHEW 6:9

Date: .... **START HERE**

Dear God, ...
....
....
....
....

I'M THANKFUL FOR. . . ..
....
....
....
....
....
....
....

MY WORRIES. . .
....
....
....
....
....
....
....
....
....
....
....
....
....
....

People I am praying for. . .
....
....
....
....
....
....

HERE'S WHAT'S GOING ON IN MY LIFE. . .

....
....
....
....
....

MY NEEDS. . .

....
....
....
....
....
....
....
....
....
....
....
....

Other stuff I need
to share with You, God. . .

66

....
....
....
....
....
....

99

AMEN.
*Thank You, God,
for hearing my prayers!*

*We always pray for you. We pray that our God
will make you worth being chosen. We pray that His
power will help you do the good things you want to do.
We pray that your work of faith will be complete.*

2 THESSALONIANS 1:11

Date: .... START HERE

Dear God, ...
....
....
....
....

I'M THANKFUL FOR. . . ..
....
....
....
....
....
....
....

MY WORRIES...
....
....
....
....
....
....
....
....
....
....
....
....
....

People I am praying for. . .
....
....
....
....
....
....

HERE'S WHAT'S GOING ON IN MY LIFE. . .

....

....

....

....

....

MY NEEDS. . .

....

....

....

....

....

....

....

....

....

....

....

....

Other stuff I need
to share with You, God. . .

"

....

....

....

....

....

....

"

AMEN.
*Thank You, God,
for hearing my prayers!*

*You answered me on the day I called.
You gave me strength in my soul.*

PSALM 138:3

Dear God, ...
....
....
....
....

I'M THANKFUL FOR. . . ..
....
....
....
....
....
....

People I am praying for. . .
....
....
....
....
....

MY WORRIES. . .
....
....
....
....
....
....
....
....
....
....
....
....
....
....
....

MY NEEDS. . .

Other stuff I need
to share with You, God. . .

"

"

AMEN.
*Thank You, God,
for hearing my prayers!*

*Trust in the Lord with all your heart,
and do not trust in your own understanding.*

PROVERBS 3:5

Date: **START HERE**

Dear God, ...
....
....
....
....

I'M THANKFUL FOR. . . ..
....
....
....
....
....
....

MY WORRIES. . .
....
....
....
....
....
....
....
....
....
....
....
....

People I am praying for. . .
....
....
....
....
....
....

HERE'S WHAT'S GOING ON IN MY LIFE...

MY NEEDS...

Other stuff I need
to share with You, God...

"

"

AMEN.
*Thank You, God,
for hearing my prayers!*

*I looked for the Lord, and He answered me.
And He took away all my fears.*

PSALM 34:4

Date: .... START HERE

Dear God, ...
....
....
....
....

I'M THANKFUL FOR. . . ..
....
....
....
....
....
....

MY WORRIES. . .
....
....
....
....
....
....
....
....
....
....
....
....
....

People I am praying for. . .
....
....
....
....
....

HERE'S WHAT'S GOING ON IN MY LIFE. . .

MY NEEDS. . .

Other stuff I need
to share with You, God. . .

AMEN.
*Thank You, God,
for hearing my prayers!*

*I want [people] everywhere to pray.
They should lift up holy hands as they pray.
They should not be angry or argue.*

1 TIMOTHY 2:8

Date: _____ **START HERE**

Dear God, ...
....
....
....

I'M THANKFUL FOR. . . ..
....
....
....
....
....
....
....

MY WORRIES. . .
....
....
....
....
....
....
....
....
....
....
....
....
....
....

People I am praying for. . .
....
....
....
....
....

HERE'S WHAT'S GOING ON IN MY LIFE. . .

....

....

....

....

....

MY NEEDS. . .

....

....

....

....

....

....

....

....

....

....

....

....

Other stuff I need
to share with You, God. . .

"
....

....

....

....

....

....

"

AMEN.
*Thank You, God,
for hearing my prayers!*

*"I say to you, whatever you ask for
when you pray, have faith that you
will receive it. Then you will get it."*

MARK 11:24

Date: **START HERE**

Dear God, ...
....
....
....
....

I'M THANKFUL FOR. . . ..
....
....
....
....
....
....
....

MY WORRIES. . .
....
....
....
....
....
....
....
....
....
....
....
....
....
....

People I am praying for. . .
....
....
....
....
....
....

....
....
....
....
....

MY NEEDS. . .

....
....
....
....
....
....
....
....
....
....
....
....

>> Other stuff I need
to share with You, God. . .

"

....
....
....
....
....

"

AMEN.
*Thank You, God,
for hearing my prayers!*

*Is anyone among you suffering?
He should pray. Is anyone happy?
He should sing songs of thanks to God.*

JAMES 5:13

Date: **START HERE**

Dear God, ...
....
....
....
....

I'M THANKFUL FOR. . . ..
....
....
....
....
....
....
....

MY WORRIES. . .
....
....
....
....
....
....
....
....
....
....
....
....
....
....

People I am praying for. . .
....
....
....
....
....
....

➤➤ Here's what's going on in my life. . .

....
....
....
....
....

MY NEEDS. . .

....
....
....
....
....
....
....
....
....
....
....
....

➤➤ Other stuff I need
to share with You, God. . .

❝

....
....
....
....
....
....
....

❞

AMEN.
*Thank You, God,
for hearing my prayers!*

*I cried out to You, O Lord. I said, "You are my
safe place, my share in the land of the living."*

PSALM 142:5

Date: **START HERE**

Dear God, ...
....
....
....
....

I'M THANKFUL FOR. . ...
....
....
....
....
....
....
....

MY WORRIES. . .
....
....
....
....
....
....
....
....
....
....
....
....
....

People I am praying for. . .
....
....
....
....
....
....

⟫ HERE'S WHAT'S GOING ON IN MY LIFE...

....
....
....
....
.... ⟫

MY NEEDS...

....
....
....
....
....
....
....
....
....
....
....
....
....
....

⟫ Other stuff I need
to share with You, God...

❝

....
....
....
....
....

❞

AMEN.
*Thank You, God,
for hearing my prayers!*

*The Father...does not respect
one person more than another.*

1 PETER 1:17

Date: **START HERE**

Dear God, ...
....
....
....
....

I'M THANKFUL FOR. . . ..
....
....
....
....
....
....
....

MY WORRIES. . .
....
....
....
....
....
....
....
....
....
....
....
....
....
....

People I am praying for. . .
....
....
....
....
....
....

HERE'S WHAT'S GOING ON IN MY LIFE. . .

....

....

....

....

....

MY NEEDS. . .

....

....

....

....

....

....

....

....

....

....

....

....

....

Other stuff I need
to share with You, God. . .

"

....

....

....

....

....

"

AMEN.
*Thank You, God,
for hearing my prayers!*

*For we belong to Christ if we keep on trusting
Him to the end just as we trusted Him at first.*

HEBREWS 3:14

Date: ‎ **START HERE**

Dear God, ...
....
....
....
....

I'M THANKFUL FOR. . . ..
....
....
....
....
....
....

MY WORRIES. . .

....
....
....
....
....
....
....
....
....
....
....
....

People I am praying for. . .
....
....
....
....
....
....

....
....
....
....
....

MY NEEDS. . .

....
....
....
....
....
....
....
....
....
....
....
....
....

" Other stuff I need to share with You, God. . .

....
....
....
....
....

"

AMEN.
*Thank You, God,
for hearing my prayers!*

*The Lord hates the gifts of the sinful,
but the prayer of the faithful is His joy.*

PROVERBS 15:8

START HERE

Date:

Dear God, ...
....
....
....
....

I'M THANKFUL FOR. . . ..
....
....
....
....
....
....

MY WORRIES. . .
....
....
....
....
....
....
....
....
....
....
....
....
....
....

People I am praying for. . .
....
....
....
....
....

HERE'S WHAT'S GOING ON IN MY LIFE. . .

....

....

....

....

....

MY NEEDS. . .

....

....

....

....

....

....

....

....

....

....

....

....

Other stuff I need
to share with You, God. . .

"

....

....

....

....

....

"

AMEN.
*Thank You, God,
for hearing my prayers!*

*Dear friends, you must become strong
in your most holy faith. Let the Holy
Spirit lead you as you pray.*

JUDE 1:20

Date:

START HERE

Dear God, ...
....
....
....
....

I'M THANKFUL FOR. . . ..
....
....
....
....
....
....

MY WORRieS. . .

....
....
....
....
....
....
....
....
....
....
....
....

People I am praying for. . .
....
....
....
....
....

HERE'S WHAT'S GOING ON IN MY LIFE...

MY NEEDS...

Other stuff I need
to share with You, God...

"

"

AMEN.
*Thank You, God,
for hearing my prayers!*

*Pray and give thanks for those who
make trouble for you. Yes, pray for
them instead of talking against them.*

ROMANS 12:14

Date: .... START HERE

Dear God, ...
....
....
....
....

I'M THANKFUL FOR. . . ..
....
....
....
....
....
....
....

MY WORRIES. . .
....
....
....
....
....
....
....
....
....
....
....
....
....

People I am praying for. . .
....
....
....
....
....

....
....
....
....
....

MY NEEDS. . .

....
....
....
....
....
....
....
....
....
....
....
....

Other stuff I need
to share with You, God. . .

"

....
....
....
....
....
....

"

AMEN.
*Thank You, God,
for hearing my prayers!*

*The Lord has heard my cry for help.
The Lord receives my prayer.*

PSALM 6:9

Date: **START HERE**

📍 Dear God, ...
....
....
....
....

I'M THANKFUL FOR. . . ..
....
....
....
....
....
....

MY WORRIES. . .
....
....
....
....
....
....
....
....
....
....
....
....
....
....

People I am praying for. . .
....
....
....
....
....

....
....
....
....
....

MY NEEDS. . .

....
....
....
....
....
....
....
....
....
....
....
....
....

Other stuff I need
to share with You, God. . .

66

....
....
....
....
....
....

99

AMEN.
*Thank You, God,
for hearing my prayers!*

*We can trust God that He
will do what He promised.*

HEBREWS 10:23

Date: _____   START HERE

Dear God, ...
....
....
....
....

I'M THANKFUL FOR. . . ..
....
....
....
....
....
....

MY WORRieS. . .
....
....
....
....
....
....
....
....
....
....
....
....
....

People I am praying for. . .
....
....
....
....
....
....

....
....
....
....
....

MY NEEDS. . .

....
....
....
....
....
....
....
....
....
....
....
....
....

*Other stuff I need
to share with You, God. . .*

66

....
....
....
....
....
....

99

AMEN.
*Thank You, God,
for hearing my prayers!*

*I am always with You.
You hold me by my right hand.*

PSALM 73:23

Date: **START HERE**

Dear God, ...
....
....
....
....

I'M THANKFUL FOR. . . ..
....
....
....
....
....
....
....

MY WORRIES. . .
....
....
....
....
....
....
....
....
....
....
....
....
....

People I am praying for. . .
....
....
....
....
....
....

MY NEEDS...

Other stuff I need
to share with You, God...

66

99

AMEN.
*Thank You, God,
for hearing my prayers!*

*O Lord, let Your loving-kindness
be upon us as we put our hope in You.*

PSALM 33:22

Date: START HERE

Dear God, ...
....
....
....
....

I'M THANKFUL FOR. . . ..
....
....
....
....
....
....
....

People I am praying for. . .
....
....
....
....
....
....

MY WORRIES. . .
....
....
....
....
....
....
....
....
....
....
....
....
....

HERE'S WHAT'S GOING ON IN MY LIFE. . .

....
....
....
....
....

MY NEEDS. . .

....
....
....
....
....
....
....
....
....
....
....
....

Other stuff I need
to share with You, God. . .

"

....
....
....
....
....

"

AMEN.
*Thank You, God,
for hearing my prayers!*

*Pray for kings and all others who are
in power over us so we might live
quiet God-like lives in peace.*

1 TIMOTHY 2:2

Date: _____ START HERE

Dear God, ...
....
....
....
....

I'M THANKFUL FOR. . . ..
....
....
....
....
....
....
....

MY WORRIES. . .
....
....
....
....
....
....
....
....
....
....
....
....

People I am praying for. . .
....
....
....
....
....

HERE'S WHAT'S GOING ON IN MY LIFE. . .

MY NEEDS. . .

Other stuff I need
to share with You, God. . .

"

"

AMEN.
*Thank You, God,
for hearing my prayers!*

For You are my hope, O Lord God.
PSALM 71:5

Date: _____ **START HERE**

Dear God, ...
....
....
....
....

I'M THANKFUL FOR. . . ..
....
....
....
....
....
....

MY WORRieS. . .
....
....
....
....
....
....
....
....
....
....
....
....

People I am praying for. . .
....
....
....
....
....
....

HERE'S WHAT'S GOING ON IN MY LIFE. . .

....
....
....
....
....

MY NEELS. . .

....
....
....
....
....
....
....
....
....
....
....

Other stuff I need
to share with You, God. . .

"

....
....
....
....
....

"

AMEN.
*Thank You, God,
for hearing my prayers!*

*"The Lord watches over those who are right
with Him. He hears their prayers."*

1 PETER 3:12

Date: **START HERE**

Dear God, ...
....
....
....
....

I'M THANKFUL FOR. . . ..
....
....
....
....
....
....

MY WORRIES. . .
....
....
....
....
....
....
....
....
....
....
....
....
....
....

People I am praying for. . .
....
....
....
....
....

HERE'S WHAT'S GOING ON IN MY LIFE. . .

....

....

....

....

....

MY NEEDS. . .

....

....

....

....

....

....

....

....

....

....

....

....

....

Other stuff I need
to share with You, God. . .

"

....

....

....

....

....

....

....

"

AMEN.
*Thank You, God,
for hearing my prayers!*

*"When you pray, go into a room by yourself.
After you have shut the door, pray to your
Father Who is in secret. Then your Father
Who sees in secret will reward you."*

MATTHEW 6:6

Date: START HERE

📍 Dear God, ...
....
....
....
....

I'M THANKFUL FOR. . . ..
....
....
....
....
....
....
....

People I am praying for. . .
....
....
....
....
....

MY WORRIES. . .
....
....
....
....
....
....
....
....
....
....
....
....
....
....

▶▶ HERE'S WHAT'S GOING ON IN MY LIFE. . .

....

....

....

....

....

MY NEEDS. . .

....

....

....

....

....

....

....

....

....

....

....

....

▶▶ Other stuff I need
to share with You, God. . .

66

....

....

....

....

....

99

AMEN.
*Thank You, God,
for hearing my prayers!*

Keep awake so you can pray.
1 PETER 4:7

START HERE

Date:

Dear God, ...
....
....
....
....

I'M THANKFUL FOR. . . ..
....
....
....
....
....
....
....

MY WORRies. . .
....
....
....
....
....
....
....
....
....
....
....
....
....
....

People I am praying for. . .
....
....
....
....
....
....

HERE'S WHAT'S GOING ON IN MY LIFE. . .

....

....

....

....

....

MY NEEDS. . .

....

....

....

....

....

....

....

....

....

....

....

....

Other stuff I need
to share with You, God. . .

"

....

....

....

....

....

"

AMEN.
*Thank You, God,
for hearing my prayers!*

*Praise the Lord! Praise the Lord, O my soul!
I will praise the Lord as long as I live. I will
sing praises to my God as long as I live.*

PSALM 146:1–2

Date: _____ **START HERE**

Dear God, ...
....
....
....
....

I'M THANKFUL FOR. . . ..
....
....
....
....
....
....
....

MY WORRIES. . .
....
....
....
....
....
....
....
....
....
....
....
....
....
....

People I am praying for. . .
....
....
....
....
....
....

HERE'S WHAT'S GOING ON IN MY LIFE. . .

....

....

....

....

....

MY NEEDS. . .

....

....

....

....

....

....

....

....

....

....

....

....

....

Other stuff I need
to share with You, God. . .

"

....

....

....

....

....

"

AMEN.
*Thank You, God,
for hearing my prayers!*

*When my worry is great within me,
Your comfort brings joy to my soul.*

PSALM 94:19

Date: .... START HERE

Dear God, ...
....
....
....
....

I'M THANKFUL FOR. . . ..
....
....
....
....
....
....
....

People I am praying for. . .
....
....
....
....
....
....

MY WORRieS. . .
....
....
....
....
....
....
....
....
....
....
....

HERE'S WHAT'S GOING ON IN MY LIFE. . .

....

....

....

....

....

MY NEEDS. . .

....

....

....

....

....

....

....

....

....

....

....

....

Other stuff I need
to share with You, God. . .

"

....

....

....

....

....

....

"

AMEN.
*Thank You, God,
for hearing my prayers!*

*I wait for the Lord. My soul
waits and I hope in His Word.*

PSALM 130:5

Date: .... START HERE

Dear God, ...
....
....
....
....

I'M THANKFUL FOR. . . ..
....
....
....
....
....
....
....

MY WORRIES. . .
....
....
....
....
....
....

People I am praying for. . .
....
....
....
....
....
....

....
....
....
....
....
....
....

HERE'S WHAT'S GOING ON IN MY LIFE...

....

....

....

....

....

MY NEEDS...

....

....

....

....

....

....

....

....

....

....

....

....

Other stuff I need
to share with You, God...

66

....

....

....

....

....

99

AMEN.

*Thank You, God,
for hearing my prayers!*

*"No one who puts his trust in
Christ will ever be put to shame."*

ROMANS 10:11

Date: **START HERE**

Dear God, ...
....
....
....
....

I'M THANKFUL FOR. . . ..
....
....
....
....
....
....
....

MY WORRiES. . .

People I am praying for. . .
....
....
....
....
....
....

HERE'S WHAT'S GOING ON IN MY LIFE. . .

....
....
....
....
....

MY NEEDS. . .

....
....
....
....
....
....
....
....
....
....
....

Other stuff I need
to share with You, God. . .

66

....
....
....
....
....

99

AMEN.
*Thank You, God,
for hearing my prayers!*

The hope of those who are right with God is joy.

PROVERBS 10:28

Date: **START HERE**

Dear God, ...
....
....
....
....

I'M THANKFUL FOR. . . ..
....
....
....
....
....
....
....

MY WORRIES...
....
....
....
....
....
....
....
....
....
....
....
....
....
....
....

People I am praying for. . .
....
....
....
....
....

>> HERE'S WHAT'S GOING ON IN MY LIFE...

....

....

....

....

....

MY NEEDS...

....

....

....

....

....

....

....

....

....

....

....

Other stuff I need
to share with You, God...

66

....

....

....

....

....

....

99

AMEN.
*Thank You, God,
for hearing my prayers!*

*God knows how I work for Him. He knows how I
preach with all my heart the Good News about
His Son. He knows how I always pray for you.*

ROMANS 1:9

Date:

START HERE

Dear God, ...
....
....
....
....

I'M THANKFUL FOR. . . ..

....
....
....
....
....
....
....

People I am praying for. . .

....
....
....
....
....
....

MY WORRIES. . .

....
....
....
....
....
....
....
....
....
....
....
....
....
....
....

....
....
....
....
....

MY NEEDS. . .

....
....
....

Other stuff I need to share with You, God. . .

..
....
....
....
....
....
....
....
....
....

AMEN.
Thank You, God, for hearing my prayers!

I love Your Law.

PSALM 119:113

Date: .... **START HERE**

Dear God, ...
....
....
....
....

I'M THANKFUL FOR. . . ..
....
....
....
....
....
....
....

MY WORRIES. . .
....
....
....
....
....
....
....
....
....
....
....
....
....
....

People I am praying for. . .
....
....
....
....
....
....

>> HERE'S WHAT'S GOING ON IN MY LIFE. . .

....

....

....

....

.... >>

MY NEEDS. . .

....

....

....

....

....

....

....

....

....

....

....

....

>> Other stuff I need
to share with You, God. . .

66

....

....

....

....

....

....

99

AMEN.
*Thank You, God,
for hearing my prayers!*

Rest in the Lord and be willing to wait for Him.

PSALM 37:7

Date: .... **START HERE**

◉ Dear God, ...
....
....
....
....

I'M THANKFUL FOR. . . ..
....
....
....
....
....
....
....

MY WORRIES. . .
....
....
....
....
....
....
....
....
....
....
....
....
....

People I am praying for. . .
....
....
....
....
....
....

HERE'S WHAT'S GOING ON IN MY LIFE. . .

MY NEEDS. . .

Other stuff I need
to share with You, God. . .

"

"

AMEN.
*Thank You, God,
for hearing my prayers!*

*I will give thanks to You, for You have answered me.
And You are the One Who saves me.*

PSALM 118:21

Date: .... START HERE

Dear God, ...
....
....
....
....

I'M THANKFUL FOR. . . ..
....
....
....
....
....
....
....

MY WORRIES. . .
....
....
....
....
....
....
....
....
....
....
....
....

People I am praying for. . .
....
....
....
....
....
....

HERE'S WHAT'S GOING ON IN MY LIFE. . .

....
....
....
....
....
....

MY NEEDS. . .

....
....
....
....
....
....
....
....
....
....
....
....
....

Other stuff I need
to share with You, God. . .

"

....
....
....
....
....

"

AMEN.
*Thank You, God,
for hearing my prayers!*

*I pray that you will know about the hope
given by God's call. I pray that you will
see how great the things are that He has
promised to those who belong to Him.*

EPHESIANS 1:18

Date: _____ **START HERE**

Dear God, ...
....
....
....
....

I'M THANKFUL FOR. . . ..
....
....
....
....
....
....

MY WORRieS. . .
....
....
....
....
....
....
....
....
....
....
....
....
....
....

People I am praying for. . .
....
....
....
....
....
....

HERE'S WHAT'S GOING ON IN MY LIFE. . .

MY NEEDS. . .

Other stuff I need
to share with You, God. . .

"

"

AMEN.
*Thank You, God,
for hearing my prayers!*

*Answer me when I call,
O my God Who is right and good!*

PSALM 4:1

Date:

START HERE

Dear God, ...
....
....
....
....

I'M THANKFUL FOR... ....
....
....
....
....
....
....
....

MY WORRIES...
....
....
....
....
....
....
....
....
....
....
....
....
....

People I am praying for...
....
....
....
....
....
....

⟫ HERE'S WHAT'S GOING ON IN MY LIFE. . .

....
....
....
....
.... ⟫

MY NEEDS. . .

....
....
....
....
....
....
....
....
....
....
....
....

⟫ Other stuff I need
to share with You, God. . .

66

....
....
....
....
....

99

AMEN.
*Thank You, God,
for hearing my prayers!*

I thank God for you whenever I think of you.

PHILIPPIANS 1:3

Date: .... START HERE

Dear God, ...
....
....
....
....

I'M THANKFUL FOR. . . ..
....
....
....
....
....
....
....

MY WORRieS. . .
....
....
....
....
....
....
....
....
....
....
....
....

People I am praying for. . .
....
....
....
....
....
....

>> HERE'S WHAT'S GOING ON IN MY LIFE. . .

....

....

....

....

....

MY NEEDS. . .

....

....

....

....

....

....

....

....

....

....

....

....

>> Other stuff I need
to share with You, God. . .

"

....

....

....

....

....

"

AMEN.

*Thank You, God,
for hearing my prayers!*

Never stop praying.

1 THESSALONIANS 5:17

INSPIRATION AND ENCOURAGEMENT
FOR GIRLS AND BOYS!

These devotional prayer books pack a powerful dose of inspiration into just-right-sized readings for 8- to 12-year-olds. Each prayer, written specifically for devotional quiet time is complemented by a relevant scripture and question for further thought.